ROB,

ENCOURAGEMENT
CAN BE FATAL —

ALSO BY MIKE DICENZO

Nothing, as of yet.

But just you wait.

There is more on the way.

Just gotta remember to write it.

Setting reminder on phone now.

"Write another book."

Done.

ENCOURAGEMENT
CAN BE FATAL
MIKE DICENZO PROSE POEMS

For Jo and Loaf

CONTENTS

The Sun 1

Chicken Liver And Pumpkin Seeds 2

Further Instruction 3

The Sacred Oath 4

Sky Writer 5

Encouragement Can Be Fatal 6

Cone 8

Avalanche 9

Trash Island 10

Implanted Memories 12

Mortal Enemy 14

Mortal Enemy, Pt. 2 15

Bounce 17

The Mime vs. The Tiger 19

Dispatches From The Middle Of Nowhere 20

The Waxy Exoskeleton Of A Babybel Cheese 21

An Otherwise Perfect Day 23

Ruins 24

The Birthday Suit Of Frederick Coates 25

Human-Like 27

A Walk In The Park 29

Leadership Summit 30

How Giraffes Get To Zoos 32

Two Mugs 33

Poem For James Tate 34

Matterhorn 35

The Cowboy And The Ferris Wheel 36

Imposter Pumpkin 38

Last Train To Goatsville 40

The Cusp Of Eternity 42

Continental Drift 44

Shadow Rebellion 45

Silent Treatment 47

Hither And Thither 49

Secrets Of The Universe 50

Two Bridges 52

Another Day On The Farm 53

Infinity Cow Shrug 54

Reckoning On 3rd Street 56

A Light In The Forest 57

An Unabridged History Of The Banana 58

Morning Constitutional 60

Interesting Jacket On A Horse 62

No One Ever Says Nucleus 63

A Distant Blinking Light 65

Strange Weekend 67

Corporate Retreat 69

The Mysterious Woman 71

The Smooth Aliens Of Mt. Vesuvius 73

The Pretty Red Bird Alighted On My Windowsill At Dawn 75

Bench 77

When It Rained In Barcelona 79

The Prayer Of Edmond Bishop 80

The Effort Of Whimsy 82

Reconnection 83

The Untimely End Of Phineas 85

One Last Sip Of Summer 86

The Reluctance Of Gravity 88

Progeny 90

ACKNOWLEDGMENTS

The Hopkins Review, in which "The Sun," "Encouragement Can Be Fatal," and "The Cusp of Eternity" first appeared.

"I looked at my watch, I looked at my wrist,
I punched myself in the face with my fist."

- Bob Dylan, *Million Dollar Bash*

THE SUN

The Sun is 1,200 miles away. It is hot to the touch. If you find yourself in a situation in which you must handle the Sun, it is suggested that you wear gloves. The thicker the glove, the better. The Sun is operated by a man named Lester Strat. He has been doing it since 1962. In the old days, he would operate it from inside the Sun. But in 1994, they switched over to remote control. It's more efficient, but it lacks the charm of those early sunrises and sunsets, which had an almost human quality. Lester is 86 years old now, and can occasionally be forgetful. Once, he left the Sun out for three straight days before remembering to set it. Another time he confused the Sun remote with his garage door opener. There is a small contingent that wants Lester dead. They long for perpetual darkness. They are the spider people, and they are coming for him. I'm in the helicopter, screaming for Lester to run, reaching out my arm as the propellers whir. But he's old, his legs… They give out, and he tosses me the remote as they pounce on him. I turn away from the carnage and shout "Go! Go!" to the pilot. One of them is hanging from the landing skids, so I kick it off and we lift away to safety. I stare down at the remote in my hand. I set my phone alarm for 5:30 a.m. The Sun will rise again. Oh yes. The Sun will indeed rise again. After a couple weeks of super-early wake-ups, I hire an intern to do it for me. Don't worry, he's very responsible, his name is Evan.

CHICKEN LIVER AND
PUMPKIN SEEDS

It had been three years since I became invisible.
I don't know how it happened, one day I just
faded away. Mary-Ellen thought it might be due
to a lack of iron in my diet. I tried eating more
chicken liver and pumpkin seeds, but my doctor
said once you're invisible there's no going back.
"Unlike a reversible jacket, it's irreversible,"
Dr. Pocket said. "That's an odd thing for a doctor
to say," I said. "No it's not. Standard medical
parlance. Now hand me that scalpel, stat!" he said.
I handed it to him, and he used it to carve open a
can of garbanzo beans. He drank from the can
and wiped his mouth with his shirtsleeve.
"Chickpea juice," he said. "Very underrated."
I went home and told Mary-Ellen the news.
She was upset and I couldn't blame her. She
came around less and less, and in that way
she became invisible, too. Last I heard she was
dating a pilot. He sounded like a good enough
guy. But if you ask me, anyone who spends that
much time in the sky must have some real issues
down here on Earth. I started going to the park
every day. I brought flowers to girls who cried
alone. I pushed children on swings. I balanced
the old woman doing tai chi. I didn't make a sound.
I was the wind.

FURTHER INSTRUCTION

The entire New York Philharmonic was standing
outside my window playing Gustav Mahler's 5th
Symphony. I yelled at them to can it, couldn't
they see some people were trying to get to sleep?
They ignored me and continued, moving on to
the Adagietto. I got up out of bed and began
hurling tangerines at them from my balcony.
One hit a cellist in the face. A second knocked the
oboe right out of the oboist's hands. A third landed
on the lawn and was hungrily devoured by the
timpani player. The bassoonists fled the scene.
The timpani player, now crawling on his hands
and knees while sniffing the ground, searched
for the first tangerine that bounced off the
cellist's forehead. Locating it, he tore off its
orange flesh and sucked the tart innards. He
inhaled it with such vigor that he began to choke.
"Hey, slow down," I called out to him. He looked
up at me with wild frenzied eyes, and bared his
teeth. He then made an otherworldly hissing
sound. I recoiled in horror. The conductor spoke.
"Don't mind him, he's just fooling around,"
he said, as the timpani player bounded into
the woods on all fours. The conductor flashed
a nervous smile, then turned and chased after him.
I went back to bed, but could not get the image
of the timpani player's eyes out of my mind. He
was trying to tell me something, I knew it. He
needed my help. But for what? I gathered the rest
of my tangerines into a leather satchel, and crept
out of the house under cover of moonlight. I headed
to the woods to await further instruction.

THE SACRED OATH

I stood in line as we took the sacred oath.
We repeated every line the leader said.
While he was talking I whispered to the
man next to me, "What is this oath for?"
He whispered, "Be quiet. You're going to
get us both in trouble." We all repeated
after the leader: "Akenamin is the one true
spirit guide, he is our life sherpa and all we
do is in service of him." I whispered, "I
think I'm in the wrong place. Is this the
Jamba Juice employee orientation?" He
whispered back, "Yes. Now shut up." After
the oath was complete, we all had to prick
our palm with a needle and place our hand
upon a glowing orb. I only pretended to
prick my palm. The man who I had identified
as the leader locked eyes with me and said,
"Ye of little faith, I cast thee out!" He was
wearing a nametag that said "Ryan." They
jeered me as I walked away, but I was glad
to be gone. I sat down on a bench. It was a
beautiful day. The leaves bent with the
morning dew. I heard the dulcet sounds of
a far-off lute, and I thought hey, someone
stole my lute! I was the only one in this town
with a lute. I found the man playing it, and
said to him, "Excuse me, that's my lute."
He played me Greensleeves and then
smashed the lute over my head. "That is
not a nice thing to do to a man's lute," I said.
"You wear it well," he said, and then skipped
off into the forest. I couldn't bear to take it
off. They called me Lute-Head.

SKY WRITER

"Sky writer seems like an insane job," I said.
"You're up there, God knows how high, in a tiny
plane, zooming all over the place, doing all kinds
of flips and flops, probably puking your brains
out, and for what? So some guy can propose
to his girlfriend, or some religious nut has got
you writing 'Jesus Loves You' up in the sky?
You've gotta have a death wish. Find another
line of work! Or if you wanna deliver messages
so bad, become a postman. Wouldn't you agree?"
"Yes," said Roberta. "Yes," said Dean. "Yes," said
Samantha. "Yes," said Jean. "Yes," said Ruben.
"Yes," said Jake. "Yes," said Lily. "Yes," said
Blake. "Yes," said Alejandro. "Yes," said Lynn.
"Yes," said Adelaide. "Yes," said Brinn. "Yes,"
said Clayton-Joseph Nunez. "Yes," said Elise.
"Yes," said Mervous. "Yes," said Denise.
I leaned back in my easy chair and chomped
on my cigar. It felt good to be a man whose many
children agreed with him.

ENCOURAGEMENT CAN BE FATAL

When I came to, I was tied to a chair. Kowalski slapped me across the face with the back of his hand, and I spit out a little blood. "Where is he?" shouted Burnside. "Where's who?" I said. I didn't know where I was or how I got there, but I recognized Kowalski and Burnside from office softball. "You know who we're talking about, Jenson. Don't play games, otherwise we might have to pluck those pretty little eyelashes of yours, one by one," Kowalski said. No one's ever complimented my eyelashes before. "Thank you," I said, "I feel like the prettiest girl at the high school dance." Burnside slapped me. "Stop playing around, or it's finger-breaking time," he said. What happened to the eyelashes, I thought. Kowalski got right in my face to the point where our noses were touching. "Where. Is. O'Donnell," he said. "I don't know," I said, "did you check with Stevens?" Kowalski and Burnside looked at one another. "Who's Stevens?" Burnside said. "Who's Stevens?! No wonder you two idiots haven't found O'Donnell, your heads are too far up your own asses to even think to track down Stevens." I had no idea what I was saying, but it seemed to be working. Kowalski looked like a sad, frightened puppy. "Look at you two standing there like a couple of warm bologna sandwiches. Untie me already!" I said. They snapped to attention and carried out my order. Some people are just lost, and they need authority figures, I thought. "Sir, are you going to help us find O'Donnell?" Burnside said. "Forget O'Donnell," I said. "We're going to the batting cages." They blindly followed me out into the cold. Snow started to fall. Street urchins sang Christmas carols.

CONE

Sometimes I walk outside with no destination
in mind. At every corner you stop and some
cosmic force tells you the way to go. Today
those cosmic forces took me to get an ice cream
cone. I ran into Kevin on my way to the river.
"Well well well, if it isn't Mr. Ice Cream," he said.
"That's me," I said, tilting my head and licking
some ice cream off the edge of the cone. "Do
you fancy yourself a tree or a mountain?" Kevin
said. "I am a mountain," I said, "unapproachable,
but admired from afar." "Trees change, they grow,
they die and are reborn, they are cut and they
bleed," he said. "I suppose we are all trees," I said,
and walked on. The river was loud. Waves crashed
upon the rocks. Tiny silhouettes walked along the
bridge. A man on a jet ski sped by and yelled, "Has
anyone seen my child?" I licked my ice cream cone
and thought back, "Have I seen any children lately?"
I was recently at a 1-year-old's birthday party.
There were many babies there, some unaccounted
for. I think one of them might have even said
"jet ski" while playing with toy blocks. I dove into
the river and swam after him, making sure to keep
my cone above the water.

AVALANCHE

The avalanche hit last Sunday. It covered the
entire town. It was strange, no one remembered
there being a mountain nearby. Yet here we are,
living under a mound of snow and ice. It's not
that different from how it was. It's colder, sure,
and darker. But aside from that, it's business
as usual. A few of the neighborhood kids have
gotten together, they plan to dig a tunnel back
to the outside world. I ran into one of them on
the street the other day. He was lugging about
seven shovels. "There's nothing for you out there,"
I said. "Sure there is, old man," he sneered.
"Like what?" I said. He dropped his shovels to
the ground. "I want to be with the beautiful people,"
he said, "glasses filled to the brim, throwing their
heads back laughing, twirling on rooftops, kissing
both cheeks. The sun shines on them even at night."
I sank back into my memory and saw flickering
glimpses. A flash of a sequined dress. The ringing
of loud music which now seems like a foreign
language but once rolled off my tongue. I grabbed
one of his shovels from the ground and said, "Lead
the way." He said, "It's going to be a long journey."
I suddenly remembered that my wife had asked
me to pick up a new tub of peanut butter pretzel
nuggets. I handed him back the shovel. "Godspeed,"
I said, receding further into the darkness.

TRASH ISLAND

In the middle of the Pacific Ocean, somewhere
between Hawaii and California, there is a
600,000 square mile floating island of garbage.
It consists largely of plastic, chemical sludge,
folded-up pizza boxes, Styrofoam instant noodle
cups, and the odd trinket here and there.
Recently anthropologists discovered a small
indigenous tribe living on the island. No one
is sure when this civilization sprang up, or
how they survive. Some theorize that the
inhabitants themselves were thrown away,
perhaps as babies, and traveled along with
the other garbage to the island. They subsist
on our food scraps, read our old books, and
play our broken instruments for entertainment.
It is a second-hand culture. But they are a
happy people, far more content with the things
we choose to discard than we are with the things
we choose to keep. Hotels have started popping
up on Trash Island. Tourists travel there to find
a missing piece of themselves, a relic from
their past. I'm walking along the shore when I
spot a familiar blue Jansport backpack. I open
it and pull out a Five Star notebook. I flip through
page after page of algebra equations. My
handwriting! Just touching it whips me back
to a moment in time, when life was simple and
concrete. "How much for this backpack?" I ask
the smiling child behind the cash register.
"$1,700," she says. "Hmm," I say and place it
back on the shore where I found it. Instead, I
just buy one of those solar-powered dancing

toys of the Garbage Monster, the delightful mascot of Trash Island. He wiggles when you put him in the sunlight. How do they get it to do that? I often wonder how things are made!

IMPLANTED MEMORIES

It started raining so I ducked into the Michael Jordan Café on Woodlawn. I spotted my friend Eleanor sitting at the counter, and she waved me over to come join her. "You're soaking wet!" she said with a laugh. "I know, it seems like it's rained every day this month," I said. "Well, take a seat! How is everything? Are you still writing?" she said. An old man eating Slam Dunk Pancakes glanced over at me. "Trying to," I said. "You know how it is." Eleanor smiled. "You were such a prolific writer in school," she said. "Ah, youth!" I said. "It's the difference between the floodgates and the faucet. Drip-drip-drip," I said. "I know, we're all getting so old. Blargh," she said. The old man again looked over at me as he doused his Slam Dunk Pancakes with a healthy pour of maple syrup. "What about you? How's your job? I heard you're working for the government," I said. "You heard right," she said. "What exactly do you do there?" I said. "Mem-Ops," she said. "I'm sorry, I don't think I know what that is," I said. "Oh, it's basically like, we go around and implant false memories into people's brains," she said. "Wow," I said, "so you're saying my family never took me to Disneyland?" Eleanor laughed. "Oh, I wish," she said, "I wish we did happy ones." A cold chill ran down my spine. "What are the memories of?" I said. "War, death, destruction, sometimes loneliness. Anything to make the way things are seem peachy by comparison," she said. "Eleanor, forgive me for saying this, but that sounds horrible," I said. "It sounds like mind control." "Well Jesus,

Tom, I'm sorry we all can't be like you and manage
a Dunkin Donuts," she said, and stormed off.
"It's actually just called Dunkin now," I shouted
after her, then softly mumbled "We rebranded…"
to myself. I looked up and noticed Old Man Pancake
staring at me again. "You look familiar," he
said. "Did you fight in the war?" "What war?"
I said. "The War of 1812," he said. "Sir, I think
that might be an implanted memory. How old
are you?" I said. "224." "Oh. Never mind."
I walked outside. It had stopped raining, or
maybe it had never started.

MORTAL ENEMY

I spotted Brendan Bristol Beck, my mortal enemy, walking down Orchard Avenue. I whistled to him, and he crossed the street. "Hello Kent," he said. "Brendan," I said. "You're looking rather gruesome," he said. "Thank you kindly," I said. "You look like you just bathed in primordial soup." "Are you implying that I resemble a primitive single-celled organism?" he said. "That is exactly what I am implying," I said. "Tut-tut," he said. "You sound like an endangered bird," I said. "Which one?" he said. "Perhaps a kakapo or a frigatebird of some sort," I said. He put me in a headlock and began walloping my skull. "I trust you are speaking of the Christmas Island frigatebird," he said. "The very same," I said, elbowing him in the guttock. "A rare and stately bird, the frigatebird. I choose to take that insult as a compliment," he said. I broke the headlock and slung him over my back in a fireman's carry. "Your shoes look like tiny leather boats," I said. "Who would sail inside them?" he asked, biting my shoulder. "Sad misshapen potatoes, or poorly painted wood dolls traveling back to their homeland," I said, dropping him to the ground. "Your facial features, when arranged thusly, evoke in me a deep sense of disgust and despair, as though your ugliness has poisoned my eyes and nothing can be beautiful again," he said, sweeping my legs and putting me in a toe hold. "Go to hell," I said. "Die, scum," he said. It's fun having a mortal enemy, it really spices up your afternoon.

MORTAL ENEMY, PT. 2

It was quiet on the bridge. Storm clouds huddled in the vast charcoal sky, and the needlepoint waves moved churchfully down the sound. My mortal enemy, Brendan Bristol Beck, had me in a full nelson. "You have the countenance of a slug," I said to him. "Are you saying I have four tentacles and a radula with 27,000 tiny teeth used to scrape and cut food before it enters my esophagus?" Brendan said. "Affirmative," I said, flipping him over my back and then junk-punching him. "Ow. Why would you punch me thusly?" he said. "I scoff at your puzzlement. You know very well why," I said. "Enlighten me," he said. "You stole my painting of a sloth sitting cross-legged on a chair and threw it into the cold, wet ocean," I said. "Codswallop," he said. He then spit on my shoe and stepped on my foot. "You have shattered my fifth metatarsal," I said. "That was the intended effect," he said. "You will regret ocean-tossing that painting. That painting was given to me by my dentist father," I said. "This is utter preposterity," he said, grabbing me by the wrist and pinching my elbow. "I did nothing of the sort to your precious painting." I tugged his ear and he yanked my hair. I gouged his eyes with my thumbs and he shin-kicked me. This tussle was far from over. The skies opened. The street vendors folded up their blankets full of jewelry and ran for cover. A clown waited under a deli awning for the bus.

BOUNCE

It was a dark and stormy day. The thunderheads loomed above the children's birthday party. I stood in the rain eating birthday cake and Sprite, stuck in a conversation with one of the moms about something called a keto diet. A few kids were running around the edge of the pool. Someone yelled, "Tyler, no!" and they all stopped. I guess they were all named Tyler. A flash of lightning split the sky in two. A second later, thunder cracked overhead. Just then, a sudden gust of wind lifted the bouncy castle a hundred feet in the air and carried it away. We watched as it sailed toward the gray horizon and disappeared out of sight. "Were any kids in there?" someone asked. "Yes," said Mrs. Fenton, "there were three. Two boys and a girl. I believe one of them was wearing yellow tube socks. Oh, the poor things! One minute they were happily bouncing, the next they were hurled as though by the gods into the unforgiving sky." Everyone had stopped listening to Mrs. Fenton and piled into a few SUVs to begin searching for the kids. We searched high and low, for hours on end, stopping only once for a quick (very quick) meal at Chipotle. Nearly fifteen hours later, we spotted the bouncy castle in the neighboring town of Haysville. We poured out of the cars and raced over. To our surprise, inside the bouncy castle were not three children, but three fully grown adults. They were wearing the same outfits as the kids, only several sizes bigger. The men had beards. But they were unmistakably the same three children from the party. One of the mothers cried out, "What happened to my little boy?!" The man in the yellow tube socks said, "In the moments since we last saw you, we have lived an entire lifetime. Full of triumphs and tragedies, sorrow, joy, pain, heartbreak, and regret." "They must've hit a time pocket," I said. Everyone nodded as if that were a real thing. It wasn't, I just made it up. But you've got to admit, "time pocket" sounds pretty good.

THE MIME VS.
THE TIGER

A mime was walking through the jungle one day when he came across a Bengal tiger. The mime froze in his tracks. The tiger crouched, coiled and ready to spring. It let out a thunderous roar. The mime, though struck with fear, stayed true to his craft and did not make a sound. Instead, he pretended to swing a lasso and toss it around the tiger's neck. As he pulled the imaginary rope back toward him, the tiger actually responded in kind, and feigned being dragged across the jungle floor. The mime then "snipped" the rope with his fingers, and the big cat, now "free," ran off. I watched this whole scene unfold through my binoculars in my bungalow. I turned to my wife and said, "Honey, you've got to see this, the most incredible thing just happened." She said, "Douglas, we need to talk." I sighed. I put down my binoculars and said, "What's wrong?" She told me she was leaving. She wouldn't be coming back. I stared in silence. "Say something," she said. "There's nothing left to say," I said. I painted my face and went out to live amongst the mimes and the tigers, take part in their little play.

DISPATCHES FROM
THE MIDDLE
OF NOWHERE

Henry Gibbs is floating in the middle of the
ocean. He has been floating there for nearly
thirty years, gently bobbing like a buoy. He
knows everything. He knows your name. If
you see him, feed him a grape. He enjoys grapes,
green grapes more than purple. Put your hand
to his mouth and slowly insert the grape. He
will not bite. He does not talk much. But if
you catch him on a good day, he will tell you
the story of his life. And oh, what a life. He
designed T-shirts and other apparel for
Looney Tunes. He made Taz what he is today.
He was tormented by his own success. So he
drifted out to sea, let the current carry him
away. Now he runs marketing for a start-up
streaming service and can sometimes be
overheard on his cell phone shouting "Content
is king!"

THE WAXY EXOSKELETON OF A BABYBEL CHEESE

I met Carlos under the bridge and he handed me the blueprints. I inspected them. Everything appeared to be in order. "Thank you, Carlos. You may go," I said. "If I may ask, sir, what are the blueprints for?" Carlos said. "If I tell you, you must promise not to be shooketh," I said. Carlos nodded. "My firm and I, we are building a new world," I said. "Wow," Carlos said. "Yes," I said. "It's a massive undertaking, very secret. No one can know. People don't like the idea of change." I drew a sharp breath of cold air. "Where will you build this new world?" Carlos said. "Right here, my good man. Right on top of the old one. It has to be done slowly, imperceptibly. You won't notice it while it's happening, but one day you'll wake up and realize everything is different than you remember. The young people, of course, will say that this is the way it's always been. You can try to argue, but ancient facts stand no chance against youthful certainty," I said. Carlos wiped his brow with a polka-dotted handkerchief. The truth can be elixir for some, and poison for others. Carlos looked flushed. I reached into my pocket and procured a round of Edam cheese. "Loose Babybel?" I said. "It's not even in its casing," Carlos said. "My pockets are clean," I assured him. "But why is it loose?" he said. "The fool asks why, while the wise man eats," I said. "Whatever, man," Carlos said, turning and walking away. An

envious rat looked on and whimpered
hungrily. "Sorry, rat. My cheese," I said to it.
I popped it into my mouth and started chewing.
To be honest, it did taste a little linty.

AN OTHERWISE
PERFECT DAY

I walked outside and sat on my front porch.
It was a beautiful day. The clouds were godlike.
Across the street, the houses stood like a row
of soldiers, each impaled with an American
flag. I sucked on a beer like it was a pacifier,
and maybe it was. The low hum of nature filled
the air. Two squirrels were in a tug-of-war
over an acorn. Countless acorns dotted the
lawn, yet they chose to wrestle over that one.
What was so special about it? They knew
something I didn't. I rapped my fingers on the
arm of my chair. I knew I had to have that
acorn. As if compelled by otherworldly forces,
I crouched and crept toward the two squirrel
friends. I moved so stealthily, so ninja-like that
I did not bend a single blade of grass. I jumped
out and shouted "Hoda Kotb!" and they dropped
the acorn and scampered away. I picked it up
and inspected it. Small. Brown. Acorn-esque.
It seemed ordinary, but I knew better. I went
inside and opened the drawer where I keep all
my other magical acorns and tossed it in. I
closed the drawer and locked it. I walked back
out to my porch. There was an army of squirrels
waiting for me. They occupied my entire front
lawn, there must have been hundreds of them,
standing on their hind legs in the ready position.
I knew this day was coming. Their leader raised
a little paw and let out a loud screech. They
began charging at me. I quickly stepped back
into a zenkutsu-dachi. Let the games begin.

RUINS

People go to Machu Picchu and stare at the
ruins. They try to imagine it when it was
bustling with life. They photograph it, to
prove that they were there, in a place where
others once were. They pose in front of the
decay to make themselves look more alive.
Climb to the top of the ridge. Look out.
See the ruins and know that someday all the
places you love will be reduced to rubble,
tourists in straw hats and fanny packs
snapping photographs, trying to imagine
what life was like then. If they squint hard
enough they can see you, riding a bike in
your backyard, laughing under bodega
lights. In their visions you're in black and
white but you remember it in vibrant colors.

THE BIRTHDAY SUIT OF
FREDERICK COATES

I went camping to clear my head, sleep under
the stars, get in touch with nature, all that
good stuff. In the woods, everything is alive.
The trees are alive. The plants, them too.
Don't forget about the bugs and the coyotes
and the great lumbering bears with their
quizzical faces and gentlemanly disposition.
It makes you feel alive being around living
things. Spend too much time indoors, you can
turn into furniture. Just ask my uncle, he's
a chest of drawers. I was lying awake when
I heard a rustle in the bushes. I grabbed my
flashlight and crawled out of the tent. "Who
goes there?" I said. A man stepped out of the
brush and into the light. I immediately
recognized him as my neighbor, Frederick
Coates. He was naked from the waist up,
as well as from the waist down. "Frederick,
what are you doing out here?" I said. "I
could ask you the same question," he said.
"I'm camping," I said. His flinty eyes flickered
in the firelight. "Have you read the Bible lately?"
Frederick said. "Yes, I read it last night,"
I said. "Isn't it good?" he said. "A classic," I
said. "Doesn't it give you all the feels?" he
said. "I wouldn't say it like that," I said. An
owl hooted. "Would you like a blanket to cover
your genitalia?" I said. "No, thank you. What's
your favorite part of the Bible?" he said.
"Probably the middle I guess, if I had to pick,"
I said. "Yeah," he said. His testicles swayed

gently in the night breeze. "I'm going to go
to sleep," I said. "Sleep can never hurt you,
and if it does, you'll never know," Frederick
said. "Good-night," I said. "Good-night," he said,
and then sprinted away. I lay down and looked
up at the stars. I thought of the creek, how it'd
be nice to go for a swim tomorrow. But then
I remembered that I left my bathing suit in
the top drawer of my uncle.

HUMAN-LIKE

There is something in my eye. Better go wash
it out, I think. I walk over to the kitchen sink
and turn on the cold water. I put my eye under
the faucet and blink. I think how this scene
might seem funny to onlookers, a human sort of
performing self-maintenance. Recently I have
seen a lot of videos of animals displaying
extremely human-like behavior. And I have to
say, I find it rather unsettling. Videos of a cat
using a door-knocker, a rat showering while
standing on its hind legs and scrubbing under its
armpits, it's all too much. I saw one where an
elephant pulled a prank on three men in a
Jeep by charging at it and then stopping at the
last second, smiling (yes, smiling!) and backing
away while waving its trunk the way a human
would wave his arm, as if to say, "Just joshing!"
I didn't like that one bit. All I could think was,
"Welp, that elephant used to be a human. There is
a human soul inside that elephant. No doubt about
it." I blink a couple more times. I can still feel
something in there, like an eyelash. I wonder, am
I that different from the animals? From a cat
licking its paw, or a bird preening its feathers?
Standing here by the sink, rubbing my eye?
Maybe the animals look at us and shake their
heads, silly humans working themselves to the
bone in tall buildings, zooming around in their
little toy cars. But still, that trunk-wave, that was
a distinctly human mannerism. Perhaps all energies
are transformative and transportative, and can
travel between all living creatures. Petra walks

into the kitchen and says, "You've been running the faucet for an hour." I look up at her, my left eye red and flushed. "I used to be an ostrich," I say. "Well, you've got the same pea-brain," she says. "Yes, and my legs. So long, so slender," I say. "What do you want for dinner?" Petra says. "I have a sudden craving for insects and small pebbles," I say. "Whatever you say, Ostrich-Man," she says. "Please," I say, "call me Brad the Ostrich."

A WALK IN THE PARK

"Beautiful day, isn't it?" I said to Helen. Helen and I were strolling through the park. "Perfect day for the park," she said. "Did you know that I designed this park, along with Lucas Dodson?" I said. "No! That's amazing! I love the fountain," she said. "The fountain was actually Lucas's idea," I said. "Oh. Well, it's all very nice," she said. An errant Frisbee landed on Helen's foot. She picked it up and flicked it back toward a group of sweaty children. "The garden path is quite exquisite," she said. "Mmm, yes," I said, "that was all Lucas." She stooped to sniff a sunflower. "The trees are all lovely, and arranged so well," she said. "Lucas did the trees," I said. "And having that quaint little foot bridge above the duck pond? Simply splendid," she said. "I'll tell Lucas he's got a fan," I said. "Say, who is this Lucas fellow? I'd like to meet him sometime," she said. Another Frisbee sailed over and landed on her foot. "Looks like I'm a Frisbee magnet!" she said. "Your shoe, anyway," I said.

LEADERSHIP SUMMIT

I was drinking heavily at the three-day
leadership summit, held at the beautiful
Solutions Provider Expo Center. A man
on stage was telling us how to start a cult
in five easy steps. The best part of the
summit was the Birds Of A Feather
roundtable, because it was essentially
just breakfast, under the guise of connecting
with like-minded individuals on common
topics of interest. "I have got a common
topic of interest for you: waffles," I said to
the man next to me as I stacked a sky-high
tower of waffles onto my plate. He didn't
laugh, but I also might not have said it
out loud. Sometimes I think things instead
of saying them. It makes life easier. In fact,
I've never said anything out loud, never
uttered a word. I'm not sure I ever will.
At this point, there's been so much buildup,
I worry that people will expect my first
words to be wise or witty. Babies can get
away with "mama" or "baba." Not me,
though. I'm going to have to say something
like "Only when you stop chasing the butterfly
will it land on your finger." Or "Those who
demand apologies are rarely satisfied by
them." Hey, those aren't half bad. Maybe
I'll say the butterfly one at the Captains of
Industry awards gala tonight. Or maybe
I'll just watch TV in my hotel room and

go to sleep. I heard there's a good dream playing tonight, the one where you go to your old apartment but the door's already ajar and everything inside is gone.

HOW GIRAFFES GET
TO ZOOS

A group of giraffes standing still is called
a tower. A group of giraffes in motion is
called a jenny. I once knew a girl named
Jenny Tower. In fact, she was my wife.
It wasn't the happiest of marriages. Things
were said, the kind of things that don't
just wash away. After a while, we grew to
resent one another, she with her thousand-
word sighs and me with my frustrated
mutterings. I still remember driving away
the last time I saw her. Moonlight scraped
the interstate. The road ahead stretched
endlessly inviting. I drove slowly, drinking
it in. A man in a sports car passed by me,
offering as a diplomatic gift his middle finger.
I said to him, "Wherever you are going, it
is better to get there late and happy than
early and angry." He said, "I am going to
the zoo." "The zoo at night?" I said. "Yes."
"Do you mind if I follow you there? I have
a lot on my mind, and I feel like looking at
animals will help," I said. "Free country,"
he said. When we got there, I headed straight
for the giraffes. How do giraffes get to zoos,
I wondered. Could it be by airplane? No, that's
silly… It's probably by boat. Yes, boat makes
most sense. Could you imagine being a giraffe
on a boat, sailing across the ocean, unsure of
where you're going, yet nonetheless praying
for fair winds and a following sea.

TWO MUGS

There are two mugs on the table in front of me. One contains poison, the other contains açaí dragonfruit melon green tea. My eyes shift from mug to mug. I ask the waiter, "Can you tell me which is which?" "I am afraid I cannot," he says, watching me with great anticipation. "This is the weirdest Cheesecake Factory I've ever been to," I say. "But if you choose wisely," he says with a deep sense of wonder, "it will be the best Cheesecake Factory you've ever been to." I reach toward the mug on my right, and his eyes widen. I pull back, and pick up the mug on my left. A bead of sweat rolls down my temple. I close my eyes and take a sip. It tastes of berries. The waiter falls into a bow. "It is of no shame to lose to a master," he says. "Wait, lose?" I say, but it is too late. He picks up the other mug and swallows its contents. "I die, humbled," he says, and then collapses onto the table. A new waiter approaches and says, "Hi, my name's Van, I'll be picking up Ko's shift. I see you're enjoying the tea, can I get you started with any apps?" "How are the nachos?" I say. "Oh, very good," he says, a twinkle of mischief in his eye. "Would you like them fully loaded?" "I believe I would," I say calmly as I reach under the table and unsheathe my katana.

POEM FOR JAMES TATE

Babies have been acting weird around me
lately. On elevators and trains, they stare
at me with a strange look of curiosity and
wonder. Perhaps they remember me from
a past life. Sometimes they offer me money.
I rarely accept it. When I do, I always say,
"Are you sure?" and "If you insist."
Yesterday a baby laughed at me. I said,
"What's so funny?" It said, "Your general
disposition." I had to laugh, because you've
got to admit, that's a pretty funny thing for
a baby to say. Sure, I was hurting on the
inside, but I try to maintain a strong outer
shell. I am like an armadillo in that way.
However, I do not subsist on insects nor am I
a prolific digger, so the shell thing is where
the comparison ends. Today a baby stopped
me on the street and asked me for directions.
"To where?" I said. "Anywhere," it said. Tears
welled up in my eyes. "I can't tell you that. I
only know how to get to the bank, and the
gas station, places like that," I said. The baby
screwed up its face. "You confuse me," it said,
and walked away on its hind legs. A nearby
baby shook its head at me and blew a mournful
note into a pan flute. Maybe they pity me, for
I was once like them. Maybe they fear me,
they know I am their future.

MATTERHORN

"I have to stop taking the rain personally,"
I said to Mildred. She bit thoughtfully into
a pear. "You're absolutely right, Norman,"
she said. "The rain falls on everyone, not just
you." The TV on the wall was playing the
Winter Olympics. Figure skaters glided
effortlessly across the ice floor. "I don't know,
I just feel like this big black cloud follows me
around everywhere I go," I said. She took
another bite of her pear. "Let's change the
subject, maybe that will help," she said.
"Okay, what would you like to talk about?"
I said. "The Matterhorn!" she said. I chuckled
at her enthusiasm and said, "What about it?"
"Well, everything!" she said. "The way it
juts out into the sky like some giant shark fin,
lurking behind tree-lined Swiss valleys. The
fact that it inspires both fear and lust. Those
who tremble before it are most compelled
to conquer its peak. Why must men climb
mountains?" "I don't know," I said, "I wouldn't
do it." "Why not?" Mildred said. "I'd be afraid
that I'd slip and fall off," I said. "It'd get you
out of your rut, though," she said. "Plunging
to my death?" I said. "Yeah!" she said with a
laugh. The back of my neck started to feel hot.
Rain lashed against the window. On the TV,
a figure skater fell down. She recovered quickly
and continued doing amazing twirls and leaps,
but it all seemed a little less breathtaking.

THE COWBOY AND
THE FERRIS WHEEL

It was summer and the carnival was in town.
Steam rose from the pavement in the church
parking lot. Children lapped at sno-cones.
When I got to the front of the line for the
Ferris wheel, the carnie said, "Sorry, sir, no
single riders." Before I could respond, a man
appeared and said, "I'll go on with you." He
was wearing blue jeans and a denim jacket
with brown leather fringe. He had a wild
mustache, and a shock of white hair poking
out from the Stetson atop his head. "Is that
okay?" I asked the carnie, who stared slack-
jawed, cigarette dangling precariously from
his bottom lip. "I guess," he said, admitting
us onto the ride. "Careful with that cigarette,
you wouldn't want it to fall out," I said as
we boarded our carriage. "Never does, never
will," the carnie said, the cigarette bouncing
up and down but, as if by magic, clinging to
his lower lip. The ride jolted as the stranger
and I started our ascent. "Are you a cowboy?"
I said. He stared straight ahead and said
nothing. We rode to the top, and the wheel
stopped to let on more passengers. Our car
swayed in the balmy breeze. "I am going to
die tonight," the cowboy said. I tightened
my grip on the ride's safety bar. "What do
you mean?" I said. No response. "Are you
on the run from the law?" I said. Without
turning his head or breaking his gaze, he said,
"Something like that." "How do you know

you're going to die tonight?" I said. "It's been written," he said. We didn't talk after that. When the ride was over, we disembarked and went our separate ways. I played the Ring Toss and won a stuffed blue monkey with really long arms. I wore him around my neck like a stole. Later on, over by the Teacups, I saw the cowboy eating cotton candy and scrolling through his phone. He looked up, but I avoided eye contact. Some people just say things, I told myself. Besides, the caramel apple stand was calling out my name, and who was I to refuse?

IMPOSTER PUMPKIN

It was a glorious autumn day and I was feeling
good. I was walking down the sidewalk in my
leather jacket, sucking on a lollipop. The sun
was shining and lovers smoked on fire escapes.
It was 3 p.m., and the bars and cafés were
filled with life. I was on my way to have lunch
with the town painter. His name was Emil. He
mostly painted flowers and haciendas. I had
a still life I wanted to commission, of a pumpkin
I had recently acquired. This was not just any
pumpkin. No, this pumpkin was almost
perfectly round. And did I mention orange?
It was the textbook definition of the color
orange. I had some pictures of it on my phone,
and I was eager to show them to Emil. In my
excitement thinking about the pumpkin,
I got slightly turned around. I unfolded my
printed-out MapQuest directions and found
my way to the Bay Leaf. Emil was seated at
a table outside. He greeted me shirtlessly, and
I told him all about my idea. I showed him
photos of my pumpkin. He gasped, then wept.
"I must paint it," he said. "This is fantastic
news," I said. "But first," he said, "I must live
with it. Observe it, absorb its essence.
Just for a few days." I shifted my lollipop
from one side of my mouth to the other.
"Deal," I said. The next day, I brought the
pumpkin and a $200 cash advance to Emil's
studio. He thanked me effusively. He bowed
to the pumpkin. "Two, three days at most,"
he said. "Take your time," I said, and left.

I never saw Emil again. I had a feeling I
wouldn't. Which is why the pumpkin I had
given him was a fake. I still have the original.
You don't let a pumpkin like that out of your
sight. Especially with All Hallows' Eve right
around the corner. This year, like every year,
I will be going as a spooky skeleton.

LAST TRAIN
TO GOATSVILLE

It was a quiet night, too quiet, yet not quiet
at all. I was sipping bourbon and gazing at
the Christmas tree, while my wife was in the
other room talking on the phone with her
senile mother. "Of course babies get haircuts!"
she screamed into the phone. "Yes Ma, bagels
have holes… Since when? What do you mean
since when, since always!" I took a very deep
sip of bourbon. She hung up and sat down on
the couch. "How's your mother?" I said.
"Lovely," she said. I choked on an ice cube.
"Don't choke," she said. "I already did," I said.
I noticed she didn't exactly spring into action.
Perhaps she secretly wanted me to die. I tucked
that thought into the back of my mind for
a rainy day, and started reading a book of poems
written by very intelligent 5-year-olds. It came
free with my purchase of a cheese danish at
Au Bon Pain. The poems were quite beautiful
and sublime, and reading them made me feel
like less of a man. I noticed my wife was looking
at her phone and smiling. "What are you smiling
about?" I said. "Cynthia posted a picture of a
goat," she said. "Since when do you like goats?"
I said. "I've always liked goats, they're adorable,"
she said. "They eat garbage, they eat cans," I
said. I was fighting a losing battle. She was on
the last train to Goatsville, and I was standing
at the station, waving my handkerchief at her
with a teardrop in my eye. When the train
disappeared out of sight, I opened up the

Goatsville brochure. There were pictures of people petting goats, feeding goats, riding goats, playing the ancient game of Mancala with goats. But wait, how could the goats pick up the stones with their hooves? I looked closer and realized that all the images were photoshopped. "Oh my God," I said. "It's a trap."

THE CUSP OF ETERNITY

Somehow I found myself on the roof with the
man about to jump. He was wearing a suit and
a tie, slightly loosened. "Don't do it," I said.
"Give me one good reason why I shouldn't,"
he said. "If you do it, you are going to die,"
I said. His tie flapped in the wind. I climbed
onto the parapet and stood next to him.
Our little town looked so pretty from up
there. The crossing guard waved at the
schoolchildren, the Pizza Hut/Taco Bell stood
defiant in its unholy union. "So, are you planning
to land on your head, your neck, your feet?"
I said. "I hadn't thought about it, to be honest,"
he said. "Are you going to do a flip? I would
try to do a flip or two, you know, put on a
show," I said. "I could make like I'm an Olympic
diver," he said. "Now you're thinking," I said.
"Say, I've never met a man who was about to
cease to exist. What's your name?" "Clyde,"
he said. We shook hands. The sun was setting.
"When you are falling, try not to think about
something stupid, like the mascot for Skinny Cow
ice cream sandwiches. You know, the very thin
cow lying on her side in a weirdly seductive
pose," I said. "Well now that you got it in my
head, that's all I'm going to be thinking about,"
he said. "I'm just saying, if I were going to
exit this mortal plane, I wouldn't want the
last thought that crosses my mind to be a sexy
cartoon cow," I said. "Stop talking about the cow,"
he said. He took a deep breath and inched closer
to the ledge. He spread his arms out wide and

42

for a second I thought he was going to fly away. We stood together in silence for the next three hours. He then carefully stepped down from the parapet, and I followed suit. "You didn't jump," I said. "I never do. I climb up here every day and stand on the ledge, just to stare nothingness in the face, feel the cold rush of eternity," he said. "You are a very odd man, but I fear I understand you," I said, and with that bade him goodnight. I went down to my apartment and opened the freezer to get a treat. I saw the Skinny Cow staring at me. "I loved you even when you weighed 1,600 pounds," I said. She smiled at me and said, "I didn't lose the weight for you. I lost it for me."

CONTINENTAL DRIFT

I was at a dinner party with Suze
and some of her friends. She was
telling a story about the time her
boss's wife gave her a colonic.
It wasn't very pleasant dinner
conversation, especially when she
was going into such great detail.
I angrily cut into my Beef Wellington.
Suze's friends were all cackling at
the story, hanging on every word.
One of them said, "How did you feel
after?" and Suze said, "Like a brand
new person." Another praised
holistic medicine. Suze said, "This
technique was actually used by the
Ancient Egyptians." I said, "You
mean the people who died when they
were 17 of old age?" Suze didn't
even hear me. She was drifting away
from me, slowly, imperceptibly. I
called out to her, but she was too
far gone, swallowed in a dizzying
sea of laughter and clinking
silverware. Even the continents
drift apart. I went to the kitchen
to clear my plate, and when I
returned, she wasn't there. The
tide had carried her off to some
far-away island of spices and rum.
I stood squinting on the shore till
sundown. Someone handed me a donut.
Someone handed me my coat.

SHADOW REBELLION

That was the night the shadows rebelled.
They split off from their human twins
and roamed the city alone, candy stores
and churches, bridges and fountains.
Some men went out to try and catch
their shadows. But the shadows were
too fast, too wily. You should have seen
old Mr. Galloway. He thought he had his
shadow cornered down by the dump,
but when he lunged at it, the shadow
flitted away, and old Galloway landed
face first in a pile of trash. The shadow
was later spotted at Beer & Co. recounting
his tale of near-capture, to the delight
of the entire bar. Summer came, and
without shadows there was no shade.
We stayed inside all day, and in that way,
we became shadows, too. A few months
later, I saw my old shadow at the bank.
I waved hello, but he was too busy
opening a Roth IRA. "I miss you," I said
through the glass. He looked up and
said, "Steven? Steven, is that you?"
We caught up over a cup of coffee. He
seemed to be doing well. He'd joined a band
("We're not great but it's fun to just get
together and jam"), took up street art
("The city is my canvas"), and engaged
in a number of brief but passionate
romances ("When I love, I love hard").
When the check came, I reached for my
wallet, but he said, "No, please, let me."

I could tell it meant a lot to him, it was
a pride thing, so I didn't put up a fight.
It was a good thing, too, since I was dead
broke, having spent my last $700 on a
really fancy haircut.

SILENT TREATMENT

Cindy hasn't spoken a word to me in four days. I wish she would tell me what's the matter, but she won't say. I suspect it has something to do with me bashing her Pilates instructor's face in with a snow shovel. "Honey, say something to me," I plead. But she just turns away and goes back to knitting a shoe for her nephew. I've gone so far as to hire a man to act as a go-between for us, but now he's giving me the silent treatment too. I suspect Cindy is sleeping with him. They even cook together. He wraps his muscular arms around her and shows her how to chiffonade Swiss chard. Show-off. I need to get my mind off Cindy, so I go to the DMV to get my driver's license renewed. "Long line, huh?" I say to the woman in front of me. "Yeah, I guess," she says. God it's good to hear another human's voice. "Sing to me, sweet angel sent from the heavens," I whisper to her. "What?" she says. "I said I hate the chip reader, I miss swiping," I say. She turns away and puts her AirPods in. I return home with my new license, feeling positive. There is a note on the table from Cindy. It reads, "I ran away with Chet. Please don't contact me. You made my life a living hell for 14 years. Screw you and the horse you rode in on." Jesus, now she's dragging Chestnut into this? Suddenly there's a knock at the door. It's Alejandro, Cindy's Pilates instructor, and he's hungry for revenge.

"I'm sorry Alejandro, this isn't a good time. Cindy left me, and I don't know what to do," I say. His expression softens. He says, "You know what will cheer you up?" I sigh. "Blasting my core?" I say. "Bingo," he says.

HITHER AND THITHER

The queen died last Sunday. The funeral was
nice, other than the part where she sat up
in her coffin and freaked everyone out. It
turned out to just be a spasm. Some people
were disappointed, they wanted her to come
back to life. Not me, though, no thank you.
I have enough to worry about in this life
without a zombie queen. I was at the Omelet
Emporium, spreading some jam on a piece
of toast, when a man dressed in all black sat
across from me. "I know you killed the queen,"
he said. "I did no such thing," I said. "Are you
sure?" he said. "Yes," I said. "Positive?" he
said. "Yes," I said. He squinted at me. "Very
well," he said. He thanked me for my
time and left. That was odd, I thought. I ate
my toast in silence, my heart racing. As I
walked home, it started coming back to me.
The fake delivery van, the shipment of wine,
the poison hemlock... "I know the queen loves
her Beaujolais," I had said to the guard. I
closed my eyes and tried to shake it all from
my memory. I took a walk to the lake to clear
my head. I looked out at the water. I saw a
great blue heron. What a funny little bird.
What a funny little world.

SECRETS OF
THE UNIVERSE

I met Lyle for a late dinner at Mr. Risotto.
He looked more depressed than usual, which
was really saying something. "How's life?"
I said. "Life is life," he said, waving a hand.
I took a sip of water. I noticed a ladybug
crawling across Lyle's face but didn't say
anything. "There's things I want to do, I just
never do them. I want to run a marathon,
I want to bench 350," he said. The ladybug
was now dangerously close to Lyle's lip.
"How much can you currently bench?"
I asked. "I don't know, I've never even tried,
and that's the point," he said. The ladybug
was now inside his mouth. "Don't go in there!"
I yelled. The ladybug heeded my advice and
crawled back out into Lyle's mustache.
"Are you even listening to me?" Lyle said.
The waiter came over with two plates and said,
"Saffron and asparagus?" I raised my hand
and said, "That's me." "And the goat cheese
risotto for you," the waiter said. "Yum,"
Lyle said. "I'm sorry for not paying attention,
I want to hear all about everything," I said.
"Can we please just focus on the risotto,"
he said. "Yes, of course," I said. Lyle took
a big bite, and then sang in an operatic voice,
"O sweet mystery of life, at last I found thee!"
"You should be an opera singer," I said.
"I am," he said. "I am Lyle Flamini, the
great opera singer of our time." "And yet
you are not satisfied, you also want to be

buff," I said. "I suppose even he who has it all still wants a little more," he said. "You have a ladybug in your ear," I said. "I know, she is whispering to me the great secrets of the universe," Lyle said. "What did she say?" I asked. "She said there are triangles everywhere, everything is a triangle if you really look," he said. I glanced around the room and counted five, maybe six triangles. After dinner, we went our separate ways. It was cold outside. I shoved my hands into my coat pockets and hunched against the wind. The streets were empty and dreamlike. I saw a pair of shoes dangling from a telephone wire. "Must not have fit," I said to myself.

TWO BRIDGES

Sometimes you can be in a groove for so long
it becomes a rut. I walked over to the two
bridges. The lights were strung across their
towers like a Christmas tree. I looked at the
carousel, the horses frozen, impaled. Their
expressions sad and mournful, their eyes
downcast. A mosquito landed on my wrist.
I decided to spare its life, like a benevolent god.
Or at least a capricious one. "All citizens must
return indoors. Five minutes until the 11 p.m.
curfew. Anyone caught loitering past curfew
will be prosecuted to the full extent of the law.
I love you, and we love America," said the Statue
of Liberty in a deep male voice, the massive
Edison phonograph inside her head blaring
this prerecorded message across the river.
People on the pier scattered and scurried back
to their homes. I dove into the shiny water
below and was surprised how warm it was.

ANOTHER DAY ON
THE FARM

I woke up in a farmhouse. I don't remember
how I got there. But the rooster was crowing,
and that meant it was time to start the day.
I wandered sleepy-eyed downstairs, and saw
a kindly farmer heaping eggs and sausage
onto a plate. "Eat up," he said. "We've got a
long day ahead of us." I was hungry, so I didn't
question him. "Did you sleep well?" he asked
between bites. "Yes," I said, "I slept for a
thousand years. I am an ancient relic, a relic
of a bygone era. I don't belong in your time."
The farmer blinked, then blinked again. The
house was so silent I could hear him blink.
"Can you please blink quieter?" I said. He
blinked again, but softer this time, which I
appreciated. Finally he spoke. "Together, we
will till the land. That is your job now, that is
what you were brought here to do." "With
all due respect, sir, I was not meant to till
the land. I am a shepherd, I herd sheep. I
am from a long time ago. I knew Jesus. How
is he? Is he doing okay?" I said. The farmer
shook his head and said, "I don't know how to
tell you this." We cried together for some
time. The sun set over the hill. The cornstalks
swayed in the night breeze. I went over to
them and danced along. For a moment, I was
one of them. I was a corn man. A wolf howled
in the distance. "Shut up, wolf!" I said. It
howled again. It wasn't going to be silenced
and I respect that.

INFINITY COW SHRUG

The gas station attendant stared at me like I
was a European candy bar. "I'm looking for
a town called Hulldale," I said. "Okay,"
he said. "My car's GPS isn't working," I said.
He stuffed some chewing tobacco in between
his lower lip and gums. "Okay," he said.
"I was wondering if you might know the
way," I said. Another car pulled into the
gas station, its tires crunching loudly on
the gravel road. "I have an important meeting
in Hulldale, sir," I said. "Oh yeah?" he said.
"What kind of a meeting?" "It is a business
meeting," I said. "And what does one do in a
business meeting?" he said. "We look at figures,
projections, sometimes numbers," I said.
"What kinds of numbers?" he said. "All sorts,"
I said. "Like, for example?" he said. "Um,
18.2, 78.9, 100…" I said. "Slow down there,
city boy, those are some fancy numbers you're
throwing around," he said. "I assure you those
numbers are not fancy," I said. "You're liable
to put someone's eye out, swinging those
numbers around like that," he said. I didn't
know what he was talking about, but I decided
to play along. "If you really want a fancy
number, try this on for size: 2,749.65,"
I said. The man's hat flew off. "Hot dog,
now you're cooking with gas," he said.
"Or how about this one: Twelve and a half,"
I said. The man's mustache, which had
previously been straight, suddenly curled.
"Boy howdy, you're frisking the whiskers,"

he said. "Hold onto your britches for this next one: Three…" I said, pausing for dramatic effect, "point three three three repeating." The man's britches fell to the ground. He extended his hand in a show of respect. He nodded at me, and I shook it. Behind him, his hat was tumbling about in the wind. "Are you going to get your hat?" I said. He turned and jogged after it, pants around his ankles. Each time he bent to pick it up, the wind sent it scurrying just out of his grasp. A man got out of the other car and walked over to me. "Seven hundred and fifty three," he said. "We are not playing this game anymore," I said. "Aw," he said, and walked back to his vehicle. A gust of wind blew the gas station attendant's hat onto the head of a nearby burro. "This ought to be interesting," I said. I opened a bottle of root beer and sat on the hood of my car to watch the show. The business meeting would have to wait, I thought. I was in the middle of nowhere, and I was starting to like it here.

RECKONING ON 3RD STREET

I was strolling through the town square, whistling
a familiar tune, when I began to notice that
everyone, every single person, was running in
the opposite direction. Naturally, I turned and
followed. Later that afternoon, I was having
a coffee with Susan. "What was all that about
earlier? What was everyone running from?"
I said. "Oh, that? That was the Reckoning," she
said. "The Reckoning?" I said. "Yep," she said,
"God came down and was tallying up sins and
doing His final judgments, all that rapture-y stuff."
"And people were running away?" I said. "Yeah,"
she said. I took a bite of my apple strudel. "Why?"
I said. "I guess they weren't ready for the end,"
she said. "Where did they go, the people running?"
I asked. "I think most went to go squeeze in a
last bit of fun, while there's still time. Some
were having picnics, playing beach volleyball,"
she said. I took a sip of my latte. "I love beach
volleyball," I said. "Spikes are fun, but me, I'm
more of a 'set' or 'bump' kind of guy." Susan
laughed as I mimed the various volleyball
motions. "So, why aren't you off having fun?"
I said. Her face fell. "I thought we were having
fun," she said quietly. "Oh," I said, setting down
my mug. "Of course." I gazed into the
foam in my latte, and I swear I saw Jesus's
face in there, winking at me.

A LIGHT IN
THE FOREST

The sun has set and I've lost my bearings.
Darkness falls upon the woods like a cloak.
I grope blindly, arms outstretched, as my
eyes strain to adjust to the night. Slowly
I begin to make out some dark shapes,
silhouettes of trees. In the shadows I see
what appears to be an infant in a baby
walker. I recoil out of instinct. "Are you
lost?" I say to it. "No," it says in a bothered
tone. "I am going to the gym, this is a
shortcut." "May I follow you?" I say. It
thinks and then says, "No. You must find
your own way." With that, it toddles off,
disappearing out of view. I lurch through
the brush for a mile or two, when suddenly
I spot something. A square of light in the
forest. It glows bright, almost too bright.
It seems unreal. I walk toward it. It appears
to be floating in the middle of the woods.
I start running directly at it. Soon a dark
cabin comes into focus around it. The light
is a window, and there's someone inside.
I slow down and tiptoe as I approach the
house. I peer into the window and see a
figure. It's the Hamburglar, and he's sad.
He's surrounded by a mountain of hamburgers,
piled high to the ceiling. He has everything
he's ever wanted. But at what cost?

AN UNABRIDGED HISTORY OF THE BANANA

Bananas used to look and taste different than they do today. What we are used to eating is the Cavendish banana. This type of banana did not exist before the 1950s. Before that, everyone ate Gros Michel bananas. However, that species of banana went extinct due to an incurable fungus called Panama Disease. Ever hear the song "Yes, We Have No Bananas"? Well now you know what they were singing about. The Gros Michels were more stout, and had a thicker peel and creamier texture. They had a stronger taste, too. Ever have a banana Runt candy? The reason it doesn't taste like the bananas you know and love is it was based on the flavor of the Gros Michel banana. Not the Cavendish. Some people still remember the Gros Michels. They insist that Cavendish bananas just aren't the same. One day those people will die, and there will be no one who remembers the Gros Michel bananas. It's sad, really. Things change, and over time people just think this is the way it's always been. Sure, banana historians will have pictures of the Gros Michels, second-hand accounts of their taste. But when was the last time you talked to a banana historian? I talked to one yesterday at my son's 12th birthday party, and let me tell you, it was pretty boring stuff. His breath smelled bad, too. I offered him a stick of gum, but he didn't get the hint. His name was Mr. Cavendish, no relation. I hope his son and my son don't become too good of friends.

MORNING
CONSTITUTIONAL

I ran into my neighbor Jerry during my morning
walk. "Jerry, what's the good word?" I said. He
said, "The pope has lost his hat." He tucked his
newspaper under his arm. "Oh no, he loves that
hat," I said. "That he does," said Jerry. "Gotta
have a hat, that's what keeps your ideas from
floating away," I said. "That's a good motto, I
shall stitch that onto a throw pillow," Jerry said.
With that, I walked on, past the elementary
school, where the children stood outside playing
games of Paper, Scissors, Rock. It was a poor
school so they couldn't afford the rights to Rock,
Paper, Scissors. I passed by the old library,
where I had sniffed many a book in my youth.
I watched a couple arguing in the park and
yelled out, "I call winner!" But when two lovers
quarrel, everyone loses, so I didn't get to play.
I sat on a bench and a pigeon landed on my
left shoulder. Following his lead, several more
pigeons flocked to me, covering my entire face
and body. A lady pushing a stroller looked at
me and said, "Now you know how I feel." I said,
muffled by pigeons, "This is how it feels to have
a baby?" "What baby?" she said. I noticed
that her stroller was not carrying a child, but an
industrial-sized container of birdseed. "This
is food for my pet pigeons," she said. "Yes,
it all makes sense now," I said. Empathy is a
rare and beautiful thing. The pigeons lifted me
up and carried me into the woods. I was tired
and thirsty so I bent down to drink some water

from a stream, when I saw it: the pope's hat.
A brown bear cub was wearing it atop his
fuzzy little head. I went to go snatch it from
him when his mother came charging at me.
I tried to explain that this hat belonged to the
pope, but I don't think she was very religious.
She swiped at me, leaving a line of claw
marks on my cheek. I ran off to alert the papal
conclave. The next morning, white smoke
billowed from the roof of the Sistine Chapel.
There was a new pope. A bear pope.

INTERESTING JACKET
ON A HORSE

Nobody's really happy, we're all just
pretending to be happy to make others
feel worse. You're not happy. You may
think you are, but you're not. That guy
over there, he's not happy either. He
wakes up every morning and goes to a
job he hates, and for what? To be allowed
to live? That woman on the subway seems
happy, laughing and talking with her
boyfriend. But watch her smile fade as
soon as he gets off at his stop. The doors
close and she turns to ash. Look at the
faces on the train. The haunted
expressions. These are souls in their
natural state. These are the spirits
wandering. It all seems too much. The
ghost of my unborn child hovers beside
me as I type, smiling and shaking his
head good-naturedly. He places a tiny
hand on my shoulder, and for reasons
unknown to me, I carry on.

NO ONE EVER
SAYS NUCLEUS

Nothing like a little turbulence to remind you
of your own mortality. This is what I said to the
man sitting next to me on the airplane. He didn't
say anything back, but he did put his headphones
on. I pressed the service light and a flight
attendant made his way over to me. "What can
I get you, sir?" he said. "I just want someone to
talk to," I said. "What would you like to talk
about?" he said. "How about the substructure
of animal cells?" I suggested. "Okay," he said,
"what's your favorite organelle?" "Hmm," I said.
"Gotta be the mitochondria." "Powerhouse of
the cell," he said, making a raise-the-roof
gesture. "You?" I said. "I'm weirdly more of
a vacuole guy," he said, putting his pinky to his
lips in a coy fashion. "Ooh, deep cut, I like it,"
I said. "All right, I've got to do the beverage cart.
Duty calls!" he said. A few moments later, I saw
him whispering to another flight attendant.
The beverage cart thing was a lie. And here I
thought I had made a new friend. Oh well, I
didn't like his vacuole answer anyway. Never
trust a vacuole man. I closed my eyes. We were
somewhere over Kansas. I kept dreaming that
I was eating food, and I'd wake up mid-bite,
chomping the air. I turned on the TV and stared
at the flight path as the cartoon plane made its
way across the United States. I realized how
many of these places I'd been to, and how lucky
I was. My story has crisscrossed the country,
jagged lines and sharp detours, scribbled from

sea to sea. Some people stay in one place all their lives, and slowly sink into the ground until they're six feet underneath it. Not me, I've hopscotched across this great land, always moving, new and exciting adventures around every bend. A woman tapped me from across the aisle and said, "Excuse me, sir, you have a sunflower seed in your beard, and it's really bothering me." I rubbed my face with both hands. "Did I get it?" I said. "No," she said.

A DISTANT
BLINKING LIGHT

"All I want to do is climb the Eiffel Tower,"
Eileen said. "Does that make me some sort
of monster?" She had been single-minded
in this quest ever since she was struck by
lightning three weeks ago. The lightning
only hit her big toe, thankfully, but the toe
was incinerated, and all that was left was
a little raisin-like nub. The doctor said the
toe would grow back, but when I asked him
was he mixing up toes and salamander tails,
he said, "Oh yeah, shoot." Eileen said, "I wish
I were a salamander," and I took her arm
and said "Maybe someday," and we walked
home in the rain. This was when the Eiffel
Tower obsession began. Her singular focus
in life was to scale the side of the famous
French landmark. I told her it was too tall.
"Why not start by climbing something shorter,
like a fire hydrant or a pyramid of canned
pinto beans at the grocery store," I said.
She stood frozen with her glass of red wine.
"You underestimate me," she said. I shivered
as the words rushed by my face. "I don't
underestimate you. I just worry about you,
with your short legs and your raisin toe,"
I said. She laughed and shook her head.
"I will climb like a bunny, you will see,"
she said. "Do bunnies climb?" I said. She
pointed up at the corner of the room. I looked
over and saw our pet rabbit Sinclair sitting
atop the bookcase. He closed his eyes and

yawned. But Sinclair was not an ordinary rabbit, was he? No, he was a Visitor from afar, watching, waiting. I couldn't tell Eileen the truth. No one could know. The fate of Earth hung in the balance. "Climb away, darling. Climb the Eiffel Tower," I said. Eileen turned into a salamander and scaled it with ease. I fed Sinclair some bok choy. He nibbled on it happily. I walked over to the window and whispered, "Soon."

STRANGE WEEKEND

I walked out to get the mail and noticed a
man camping out on my lawn. It looked like
he had slept there. When he saw me, he jumped
up and pointed at me. "You're him!" he said.
"Who are you?" I said. "I'm your number one
fan!" he said. "Can I get a selfie?" It seemed
dangerous to say no, so I obliged. I didn't
know where he knew me from or why he
was a fan. The next day, I was out to dinner
at Yosef's. People were taking surreptitious
photos of me. They were holding their phones
at odd angles, pretending to squint at emails
or texts, but I knew they were photographing
me. The waiter came over carrying a large
brownie and said, "Dessert for you, compliments
of the chef." I said, "No, I couldn't, I didn't
order this, and besides I'm full, full, thank
you, but full." He said, "Will break chef's
heart if you don't at least try." I said, "Please,
no, if I eat one more bite I'll explode, tell him
everything was delicious. And I'll take the
check." I was getting a little irritated. The
waiter came back with the brownie and said,
"Sir, the chef said to inform you that if you
don't try the brownie, he will kill himself. He
said he has been thinking about it anyway,
and that this would push it over the edge.
He said it's ultimately up to you, but that
he is serious, he will take his own life."
I forked a corner of the brownie and put it
in my mouth. "Yum," I said angrily. "Check?"
He said, "No, no, for you? On the house."

I said, "Well, at least let me tip you." He said,
"No, no tip. But can I get a photo with you,
for my kids?" "For your kids?" I said. "Yes,
Henry and Sadie," he said. I closed my eyes
and breathed a long breath. "Okay, let's do
it," I said. "Here," he said, handing his phone
to a short man in a vest. He put his arm around
me and gave a thumbs-up. "Now one with the
flash," he said. "Now one vertical," he said.
"Good to have options," he whispered to me.
I walked home in the freezing cold. Lights
turned on in the houses as I passed them.
I saw my number one fan asleep in my yard.
I nudged him awake with my foot. "Why are
you a fan? How do you know me?" I said.
"Dude, your epic viral skateboard trick video,"
he said. "Oh, that," I said, and went inside.

CORPORATE RETREAT

Two businessmen in inner tubes float down
the lazy river. A bird imitates the sound of a
jackhammer. I stagger around the rainforest
floor, looking for Damien Powers, my assigned
"buddy" on this corporate retreat. The jungle
is alive and the sun is going down. A procession
of elephants returns from a funeral. A three-toed
sloth slowly dances for my amusement. I toss
him a crinkled dollar bill, I don't have time
for this right now. I have to find Damien and get
back to camp before darkness falls and the
creepy crawlers come out. A tapir lifts its
head from a shallow swamp and blinks dumbly.
I spot a jaguar hiding in a tree, and he puts a paw
to his lips to shush me. I nod. His secret is safe
with me. If all else fails, if I get lost in here and
have to live in the wild, I can become the jaguar's
courtier. His loyal servant, his eyes and ears.
"Where did that capybara go? I would like to
eat him for dinner," he would say to me. "I shall
inquire as to his whereabouts, sire," I would say
calmly. But inside I would be panicking. I'd be
running around the jungle, bribing the local
macaw with an offering of nuts and seeds in
exchange for information about the capybara.
I'm not cut out for these games of power. I'm
no Lord Talleyrand; I'm no Otto von Bismarck.
I hear a voice call my name. It's Damien. "Where
have you been?" I say. "I was over by the pond,
there's a bunch of capybara hanging out over
there," he says. My ears perk up. "Which pond?"
I ask Damien. "It's about a mile north of here.

I was there with Coleman and Morris," he says. "Interesting," I say. I glance up to the jaguar in the tree. He nods. My position in his kingdom is secure. For now...

THE MYSTERIOUS
WOMAN

I was enjoying a light breakfast on the hotel
rooftop, looking out at the serene ocean water,
when a woman sat down across from me. "Do
you remember me?" she said. I studied her
face. "Veronica?" I said. "No," she said. I
removed my sunglasses and squinted. "Trista?"
I said. "No, not Trista," she said. I frowned.
"Could you be Fatima, the lawyer's daughter,
all grown up?" I said. "No, but you are getting
warmer," she said. I thought for a moment.
"Aha! Jocelyn! Is that you?" I said. "Now you
are way off," she said. "Can you give me a hint?"
I said. "That would ruin the fun," she said.
Some fun. "Pauline?" I said. "Not Pauline,"
she said. "Are you Eve, with whom I shared a
kiss in the crown of the Statue of Liberty?"
I said. "I am afraid I have never been to the
Statue of Liberty," she said. "Oh, you should
consider going sometime, it's really quite
magnificent," I said. "Let's get back to the
guessing, shall we?" she said. "Angeline?" I
said. "No," she said. "Wait, I know you. You're
Genevieve, the princess of Luxembourg," I
said. "Not quite," she said. I had never seen
this woman before in my life, I was sure of it.
But I was determined to win her twisted game.
"Are you Henrietta Finch, the chief gentlewoman
of the privy chamber?" I said. "I am indeed," she
said. She clapped her hands politely. "So you
remember, then?" "How could I forget?" I said.
"The midnight stroll by the lake, the junipers in

full bloom, the wind whispering as your hand grazed mine, our fingers intertwining..." Of course, I was making all that up. None of it actually happened. Although, the more I thought about it, maybe it did. Yes, it was all coming back to me, like an ancient dream. The scent of the junipers, the caress of the breeze. Memories can be implanted. Entire false histories can be constructed. I gazed out at the sea. A silver dolphin leapt from the crystal blue water and landed in my grapefruit juice. I took a bite of my Cap'n Crunch and nearly shredded the roof of my mouth.

THE SMOOTH ALIENS
OF MT. VESUVIUS

In the department store, a man places a wool
cap onto a mannequin. "It's better when they're
not bald," I say, giving a thumbs-up. Startled,
the man whips around and grabs his chest.
"You scared me," he says. "The hats make
them look more human. Without them, they
look like smooth aliens, or some kind of race
of fossilized people, like the ones frozen in
time by the volcanic ash of Mt. Vesuvius,"
I say. "That's the third time today someone's
brought up Mt. Vesuvius," he says. "That is
shocking to me," I say. I pick up my bag filled
with colorful socks that I purchased for my
children and walk on. I pass by a few more
mannequins. They stare at me with their
faceless, eyeless faces. I quicken my pace,
and begin to slowly jog. Soon I am sprinting.
I hear footsteps behind me. I wheel around,
and there in the middle of the aisle, I see
three child-sized mannequins, frozen in a
playful running motion. They are approximately
the same age and height as my own children,
and they are dressed in clothes that I swear
I've seen my children wear. I text Alice,
"Where are the kids?" My phone starts ringing.
It's Alice. "Hello?" I say. She is yelling.
"What do you mean where are the kids?
The kids are with you, you brought them to
the mall!" I sit on the floor and put my phone

down. The room spins. I look at the mannequins.
They have no faces, but I can tell they are
laughing, they are happy. I weep as I slide
socks onto their smooth alien feet.

THE PRETTY RED BIRD ALIGHTED ON MY WINDOWSILL AT DAWN

The pretty red bird alighted on my windowsill at dawn, and I was immediately struck with a deep sense of foreboding. The bird had a puffed-out chest and a crown of feathers. It was clear that he was better than me. I closed the curtains, I did not want him to see my modest home. He had no business here, there must've been some sort of mix-up down at bird headquarters. He belonged in a palace, perched atop the shoulder of a king or Jared Leto. I started to feel uneasy, so I got in my car and sped over to the pub, blowing through every stop sign and red light on the way. It's a wonder I didn't kill anyone, and only lightly grazed seven. The barkeep bellowed, "What'll ya have?" in his signature Irish brogue. "Give me one of everything," I said. He said, "One drink at a time, mate," so I said for him to give me his cheapest whiskey mixed with his most expensive ginger ale. Just then, the pretty red bird alighted on the barstool next to me. From this angle, the bird resembled Margaret. "Margaret?" I said. The bird pecked "Yes" in Morse code onto the stool. I could tell there was a message she wanted to get to me. I hushed the bar. I repeated out loud as she pecked, "It wasn't the happiest of relationships, but you taught me to be confident in myself. The lessons

I learned made me who I am today: a smart, strong, and successful woman." The pecks stopped. Tears welled in my eyes. The bartender blew his nose on a rag. "That was beautiful," he said. "This one's on the house." He handed me a Heineken keg can. "Wow," I said with a sniffle, "it's shaped exactly like a keg." "That's why they call it a keg can, mate," he said. When I looked back at the barstool, the pretty red bird was gone, no doubt somewhere exotic, no doubt being fed grapes by Jared Leto.

BENCH

A stranger sat beside me on a bench. "Hello,"
he said. "I am an alien from another planet."
"Hello," I said, "I am Jeffrey from this one."
We sat in silence for three to four moments.
"I wish to know more about your kind," the
alien said. "May I ask you some questions?"
"Shoot," I said, setting aside the issue of
Chickens Magazine I was perusing. "Question
one: What is a scone?" the alien said. "A scone?
It's like a little cake pastry type thing, like
for breakfast and stuff," I said, sort of struggling
to define it to be honest. "Question two: What
is the best kind of scone?" he said. "Um, I
guess blueberry?" I said. "You guess or you
know?" he said, sounding a bit agitated. "Taste
is subjective here on Earth," I said. "Fine," he
said. "Last question: How do you procreate?"
(This was more the line of questioning I was
expecting). I said, "Well, when a male loves a
female, he puts his 'penis' inside her 'vagina,'"
I said, unsure why I was making air-quotes
when saying the anatomically correct terms.
"His sperm fertilizes her egg, and then nine
months later, a baby comes out." Suddenly the
alien removed its mask and unzipped its body
to reveal it was not an alien at all, but my
13-year-old son. "Thanks for telling me about
the birds and the bees, Dad," he said. I admit I
was slightly relieved to have gotten "the talk"
over with, but I was somewhat hurt. "Did
you really feel you couldn't come to your

father, man to man?" I asked. He smiled but did not answer. "And why all the questions about scones?" I said. He said, "I was just curious."

WHEN IT RAINED
IN BARCELONA

I dipped into a small café. Every wall, curtain, and
tablecloth was bright red with gold floral patterns.
They were playing Christmas music in March,
classical renditions of "Jingle Bells" and "How
Great Thou Art." I ordered a sweet chai tea and
a manchego sandwich. My Spanish was not great.
Mostly I pointed at things, like a smart ape. The
waiter came over and asked was everything good.
I said yes. I could've said "si," but why live a lie.
I didn't speak Spanish and he knew it. I think he
respected me for not pretending. I hope he did,
anyway. The respect of strangers in foreign lands
means everything to me. I sipped my tea and gazed
out the open door of the café. Rain splashed on
cobblestone streets. Couples hurried by sharing
umbrellas. I read about ghosts and Bob Dylan.
How one time on a track, he accidentally sang
the word "stadows" instead of "shadows." The
sound engineer used a different take for the mix,
but Dylan insisted he go back to the "stadows"
take. Finally, the guy worked up the courage to tell
Dylan, "On that take, you say 'stadows' instead
of 'shadows.'" Dylan responded, "Yeah, well,
you know. Stadows." I laughed to myself, and
everything felt okay for a moment. And it's
moments like those when you realize how rarely
things feel okay. After a while, the rain let up.
I paid my bill and left. A man outside was
playing the saxophone, and the notes, I could
see them, they rose like steam from the bell
of the silver beast.

THE PRAYER
OF EDMOND BISHOP

I met Edmond Bishop a few years ago at a
build-your-own-moss-terrarium workshop.
We became fast friends, largely due to
our shared interest in moss terrariums.
"You can create your own little world, be
a god," Edmond would say. I would laugh
a little, because hey it's just moss, though
secretly I did come to view him as a god,
and worshipped him, and made a small
porcelain figurine in his likeness that I
prayed to nightly. I wasn't fanatical or
anything, and later only really worshipped
him on Christmas and Easter, Christmas
coincidentally being his birthday and
Easter being the day he rose from the dead.
Edmond used to be an astronaut. I had a
weekly lunch with him where I picked
his brain about outer space. "Do you really
float around up there?" I said. "All the
time," he said. "What do you eat in space?"
I said. "Mostly pierogis," he said. "Living
the dream," I said. "You got that right,
mister," he said. "Where is Jupiter?" I said,
dunking a french fry in Thousand Island
dressing. "Jupiter is very far away," he
said, eyeing my fries. "Have some," I said.
"I couldn't," he said. "I insist," I said. He
hesitated, then said, "Well, if you insist."
He daintily picked up the smallest fry on
my plate, a nub really. "You can do better
than that," I said. He grabbed a fistful

of fries and shoved them into this mouth, loudly chewing and proclaiming, "I'm the Fry Monster!" It was very unlike Edmond, and I began to question whether he was a god, or just a very lost human being. I picked up the check and we walked outside. "Well, I'm going this way," I said. Edmond said, "Hey remember when I was the Fry Monster?" I said, "No, I don't recall," and walked off. Later that day, Edmond died. I could feel my faith slipping. I put my porcelain figurine of Edmond in my pantry behind a bag of Salt Twists. A few days later, I was out walking my dog, and I spotted Edmond in the town square, giving money to a street juggler. I breathed a deep sigh of relief. The juggler and the messiah, together again.

THE EFFORT
OF WHIMSY

"You aren't as whimsical as you used to be," Clara said. I brow-furrowed skeptically. "Whimsical?" I said, rapping my fingers on my thigh. "When was I ever whimsical?" "I don't know, you were just… more spontaneous, is all," she said. I mouth-frowned. "Well, I don't know, Clara, what do you want? You want me to put on clown pants? Do an impromptu flugelhorn performance?" I said. "That would be nice," she said. I stomped down to the basement to get my flugelhorn. I spotted it by the toolbox. I made as much of a racket as I could getting it off the shelf, rattling the toolbox drawers and even dropping a wrench or two, to show that I was mad through sound-noises. I trudged back up to the kitchen with the flugelhorn and blew out some jazz improvisation in F-major. Clara clapped. "You're like a young Chuck Mangione," she said. "There, are you happy?" I said. She said, "Now do the clown pants." I sighed. Back down to the basement I go! It never ends!

RECONNECTION

I was walking along the waterfront at dusk
when I spotted a king sitting alone on a large
rock. His iridescent crown sparkled in the
setting sun. I approached him carefully, for
fear that he might bite. "May I sit beside you
on this rock?" I said. He turned toward me,
his sad eyes like saucers. "Sit, my son," he
said. "…Dad?" I said. He nodded. "I have
so many questions," I said. "The only thing
worse than a question unanswered is a
question unasked," he said. "Why did you
leave?" I said. He sighed. Then he held out
his hand and a bird landed on it. I considered
snapping a quick photo and posting it with
the caption "Reconnected with the parental
unit this weekend. My dad's a king now and
can summon animals. #BoatTailedGrackle."
But out of respect, I didn't. The king tilted
his head and said, "Just as birds must leave
their nests, so too must men." "What are
you king of?" I said. "A small empire overseas,
you've probably never heard of it," he said.
"Try me," I said. "Spain," he said. "Of course
I know Spain." "Not that one, a different
Spain," he said. "Oh," I said. "Does this mean
that I am a prince?" "Sort of. But I have two
children with the queen, you should meet
them sometime, their names are Jonathan
and Pillow. I also have a pet chicken named
Tomás who technically outranks you in the
royal line of succession, and would therefore
become king before you," he said. "A chicken

king?" I said. "He's actually quite smart. He can add and subtract using corn, and once I thought I saw him reading Infinite Jest," he said. "Wow," I said. "He wasn't, but still," he said. "Yes, but still," I said. I understood. "Are you going to stay?" I said. "I am afraid not. My people need me," he said. Church bells rang. He flapped his arms and flew off toward the sun. My father, the Chicken King.

THE UNTIMELY END
OF PHINEAS

I hit the snooze button for an hour. In
between, I dreamed I was a pirate, having
adventures on the high seas. I had a parrot
on one shoulder, and a devil on the other.
They both repeated everything I said.
A mischievous beaver in an overcoat
gnawed on my leg of peg. Me and the
other pirates searched for treasure
buried in bottoms of bottles. "Land,
ho!" I said, and we crashed into my old
high school. I hadn't gone to my English
class all semester and today was the
final exam. Even though I had slit the
throats of innocent men in pursuit of
gold, I was nervous and didn't want to
fail. I sharpened my pencil and without
thinking wrote, "The hard marble steps
in 'A Separate Peace' symbolize the
callousness of life." The pencil tip snapped
and I woke with a start. I looked at my
shoulder. The parrot was gone, but the
devil was still there. I asked him, "What
happened to the bird?" The devil said,
"He flew directly into the jet engine of a
747." "Oh my God, who was piloting the
plane? I hope it was Sully Sullenberger."
"It was." "Thank goodness."

ONE LAST SIP
OF SUMMER

It wasn't until later that I discovered the
stone had magical powers. I thought it was
just a stone, a stone given to me by a decrepit
old woman on the street, who pressed it
tightly into my palm with two icy hands
and whispered, "This stone can bring you
great fortune, but also great misery," then
disappeared into the crowd. I assumed she
was a lunatic, but I kept the stone because
hey, free stone. For years it just sat there
in my desk drawer, not bringing me any
great fortune. It might've brought some
misery, but looking back, I probably brought
that on myself. Then one day, I picked up
the stone and said, "I wish I had a cream of
tomato soup right about now." Do you know
what happened? Not five minutes later, my
coworker Danny Kite stopped by my cubicle
and said the woman at Soup Cave accidentally
gave him two cream of tomatoes and asked
did I want one. I looked at the stone and said,
"Son of a gun, you've been holding out on me."
For the next two years, I exclusively used the
stone to get free soups from Soup Cave. But
then I started branching out with bigger
requests. Remember when the kids from
the movie "The Sandlot" reunited and played
catch? That was me and the stone. Life was
good. Sure, things weren't great between
me and Carla, but there are some things
even magic can't fix. She grew jealous of

the stone, said I was spending too much time with it. I told her to relax, it's just a talisman. She said she didn't like my tone and maybe I should wish for a new wife, so I did just that. Soon after, a young woman with wet hair rang the doorbell. "Are you the new wife then?" I asked. She said, "No, I just got fired from Soup Cave for mixing up over 600 orders the past three years, and I hear you are the one responsible." Carla cackled loudly as she rolled her suitcase out the door, flipping me off and saying, "Have a nice life, Weasel Boy." Which is funny, because she'd never called me that before. Another funny thing is that the stone worked after all, since me and the Soup Cave girl ended up getting married. Her name was Abigail. It was a bright September day and the sun shone down on the whole congregation. The stone was my best man, looking quite dapper in a velvet shawl-collar tuxedo.

THE RELUCTANCE
OF GRAVITY

It was noon at the Panini Hole, which meant
Chuck was half an hour late. To pass the time,
I read the back of a sugar packet. Nutritive
dextrose. You don't say? Finally, Chuck walked
in, looking rather perturbed. "What's the
matter?" I said. "The birds, they're falling,"
he said, slightly out of breath. I said, "What do
you mean they're falling?" "They're falling
out of the sky, thousands of them," he said.
"Come, see for yourself." He led me outside,
and sure enough, he was right. The sky was
dotted and streaked with countless birds
hurtling toward Earth as though they had all
simultaneously forgotten how to fly. "Well
that's not ominous at all," I said. A crowd had
gathered. Everyone's heads were tilted
toward the sky. "Do you think this signals the
End Times?" Chuck said. An old woman
wearing a babushka scoffed and shook her
head. "I've seen this happen twice before,"
she said, waggling a crooked finger. "First in
1942 and again in 1957. In Eastern cultures
it's actually a good luck omen, a sign from
the gods that the upcoming Spring will bring
forth a bountiful harvest." "Is that true?" I
said. "No," she said. "Then why did you say
it?" I said. "People tend to believe whatever
I say because I am old and mysterious. But
the truth is I'm really quite lonely. And this
babushka isn't even mine, it's a rental."

I looked at her with pity as an osprey plunged
headlong onto the roof of a Nissan Sentra.
"Let's go inside and eat," I said to Chuck.
"Feel free to join us," I said to the old woman,
but she had disappeared like sand in the wind.
Either that, or she just walked away.

PROGENY

Little a turned to Big A
and said, "Why are you tall
and pointy, and I am short
and round?" Big A pretended
to be asleep. Little a said softly,
"You're not my real dad,
are you?" Meanwhile, Big D
glanced around nervously.
"Time to find a new town,"
he said to himself. He picked
up his firstborn and left the
alphabet.

The en.